The World According to Evan Mecham

A collection of quotes, observations and editorial cartoons

"Mecham, Me See, Me Conquer"

by
Dr. Mark Siegel

Cover Illustration by Rand Carlson

First Printing
October 1987

On Misquoting Mecham
Some Thoughts For Those Who Need a Rationale for Reading Cartoons
(others can skip to page 11)

> "Conscience: That inner voice that tells us someone may be watching."
>
> A filler from *The Governor's Report to the People of Arizona*, September 1987

There is no doubt that Evan Mecham is misquoted by the press. *Newsweek Magazine's* assertion that Mecham once called Eisenhower a leftist is undocumented, for instance; it may stem from a debate in which Mecham maintained that even the Eisenhower presidency supported inherently socialistic programs, or it may come from a series of quotes from other sources that Mecham incorporated into his book, *Come Back America*. For example, Mecham writes: "In the *Congressional Record* for April 17, 1958, Norman Thomas is quoted as saying:

> 'The United States is making greater strides toward Socialism under Eisenhower than even under Roosevelt'" (p. 61).

Because Mecham doesn't say if he agrees or disagrees, and the quote supports his own argument, the reader might logically assume that Mecham shares Thomas's opinion. Yet, in early September 1987, when confronted by a caller on his radio talk show who repeated the phrase from *Newsweek*, Mecham vehemently denied having called Eisenhower a socialist, and blasted his antagonist as both a victim and a purveyor

1

A BORO SELF-PORTRAIT: *Working on a Gov. Mecham cartoon that promotes the appearance of fairness.*

BORO *The Phoenix Gazette '87*

of false information. Here and at other times when Mecham has tangled with the press, the pertinent question is not just "Has he been misquoted?" (Yes he has), but also, "Has he been misrepresented?"

Isn't he responsible for the implications that can be drawn from what he says?

To answer that question, you have to read Mecham yourself. Hence this handy book of quotes. They are all taken out of context, and therefore subject to distortion. No attempt is made to excuse or portray these statements in their best light—after all, the governor has television and radio talk shows and his own sporadic publication to accomplish that end. Anyone, even Evan Mecham, can look good at his best. But it's difficult to give full credit to a governor who can say, with a perfectly straight face, "We'll always answer questions, but we'll choose the questions" (*The Arizona Republic*, October 1, 1987). Does this guy think he's a character in *Alice in Wonderland*, or what?

Mecham is capable of restraint, or even fatherly patience. Yet suddenly there is a flash of anger, real pugnacity that sometimes descends to the most childishly malevolent innuendo, and the distinguished governor is accusing Recall Leader Ed Buck of being on someone's secret payroll and labeling Recall organizers "a band of homosexuals and a few dissident Democrats." (Perhaps the governor would rejoin, "I never said anything like Buck was on anyone's secret payroll. I merely said, 'I don't know who's paying him.'") The astonishing thing about Mecham's rhetoric is his unmitigated self-righteousness and self-assurance in attacking people who oppose him. Reporters who anger him become "nonpersons," apparently excommunicated from society, unfit for existence on the governor's planet. (Issues that he finds particularly aggravating, like Martin Luther King, Jr., Day, have sometimes become "non-issues," and, with any luck, this volume will officially become a "non-book.")

One amazing example involved entertainer Ben Vereen, in Tucson to do a benefit for the American Cancer Society. Simply because Vereen spoke out in favor of a state holiday commemorating Martin Luther King, Mecham accused him of pocketing money from the concert. When a spokesperson from the ACS assured reporters that all funds were accounted for and that Vereen had appeared gratis, Mecham merely chuckled, "I hope you force him to give it all to the Cancer Society instead of him taking a pretty good piece of it home for his bank account. I know these people like the palm of my hand" (Associated Press).

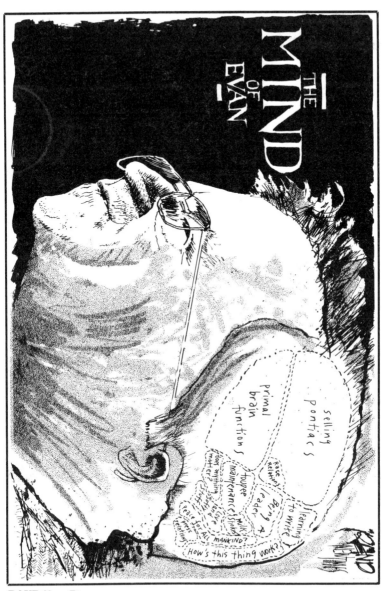

BORO *The Phoenix Gazette '87*

Evan Mecham claims to be a straight-speaking man, a man whose only flaw may be that he speaks out courageously what others only dare to think. In fact, one of Mecham's favorite devices is to speak *for* those nameless others:

> "Some feel that there was a great conspiracy [in the 1970s] to kill off the U.S. car industry in order to kill the U.S. economy. Out of the resulting chaos the Socialists would finish destroying the Republic and emerge with a Socialistic Dictatorship in complete control."
>
> *Come Back America*, p. 74

While one might be skeptical about Ev's professed knowledge of show-biz people like Ben Vereen, the guy's been a Pontiac dealer for years and ought to know about the car industry if he knows about anything. And Ev assures us he wouldn't speak without proof:

> "Without proof I wouldn't accuse the Japanese of being good payoff artists, feeding the car buff magazines and some of the American press so that the attack on American-made cars reached gigantic proportions, but it makes me wonder."
>
> *CBA*, p. 74

Remember, you folks given to misquoting, Evan Mecham *said* he wasn't necessarily saying the things he just said.

The other big thing that bothers the governor about his misquoting critics (besides their lifestyles and their morality) is that they say so many things about him and his staff without any proof. "Why don't they say something factual?" he complained to a reporter from The Associated Press. In his own writing, Ev often makes a distinction between theory and fact. One theory on the plight of the American auto industry in the early 1980s was that it was intelligently marketing a competitive product but was the victim of the Socialist Conspiracy, served by labor unions and environmentalists: "The decline of the U.S. auto industry which spearheads the economy raised the question: Was this planned destruction or the result of bureaucratic intervention?" (*CBA*, p. 69). Facts, on the other hand, are apparently what follows:

> So-called 'environmentalists' were encouraged and given so much government help that it became impossible to build refineries in the U.S. to meet the nation's fuel requirements. It appeared that the Master Planners decided the other sure way to bring America to her knees was to make us dependent on foreign sources of energy. To help this along, nuclear energy, originally developed in the U.S., made much more progress abroad because of government, ecologists, and soft-headed judges. . . . [Ditto coal and oil.] These actions were what allowed OPEC nations to hold America hostage and start the transfer of much of the world's wealth from the industrial nations who created the wealth to people who never knew what oil was until Western technology went and developed it for them. . . . If the facts were to be published as a fiction story it wouldn't sell because it would appear too preposterous. (*CBA*, p. 76)

Judging from the response of editorial cartoonists, journalists, and other politicians, the "facts" themselves of Mecham's administration frequently have seemed more than a little preposterous. What I've done here is to juxtapose some of those facts to the exaggerated interpretations provided by editorial cartoonists, so that you can draw your own conclusions about the ultimate implications of the governor's remarks.

This volume presents a collection of quotations from Governor Evan Mecham and his staff, and the reaction of editorial cartoonists from Arizona and, occasionally, one of those agitating Eastern liberal bleeding-heart "rabid left-wingers who really want to give me a rash," as the governor said in *Newsweek*. So remember, *I* didn't say these things.

FITZSIMMONS © '87 The Arizona Daily Star

I.
What's So Funny?

"I'm everybody's friend."

Arizona Trend,
January 1987

Evan Mecham spent two years in the Arizona State Legislature in the 1960s. He dabbled in newspaper publishing, ran a successful Pontiac dealership in Glendale, Arizona, and maintained a recognizable profile in Arizona politics by losing races for the United States Senate and four shots at the governorship. On his fifth attempt, in November of 1986, he was elected governor of Arizona by garnering 40% of the vote in a three-way battle royal with Democratic candidate Carolyn Warner and Independent (formerly Democrat) Bill Schulz.

Certainly he might have won in a two-way race, and, even if the current recall drive against him is successful, he may win the same fight again in April 1988. However, in the meantime, Evan Mecham has managed to make himself one of the most controversial — and, many people seem to feel, one of the most entertaining — figures in American politics. The Recall movement against him began virtually before he took office, though state law postponed for six months the official start of the petition circulation, which will require 25% of the total vote cast in the original election (approximately 220,000 signatures) to force a reelection in April of 1988.

An opinion poll conducted by the Arizona Republic on May 15, 1987, showed only 38% of those polled to be satisfied with the governor's performance, and listed him second, one percentage point behind drugs and tied with rapid population growth, as the most serious problem facing Arizona. On the other hand, as Mecham was quick to point out, this is the same poll that showed him losing both the primary and the general elections by large margins.

In any event, in the meantime, Arizona's got Mecham. And vice versa. As he's explained,

> "The image that I think we have is that Arizona is a place where people can speak their minds, and they have a governor who does that."

> *The Arizona Republic*
> March 3, 1987

> "Arizona is ready to get into the big time."

> *Arizona Trend,*
> January 1987

BORO *The Phoenix Gazette '87*

BORO *With Apologies to Hart, Davis, Trudeau, Wisewite, Larschboro The Phoenix Gazette '87*

Q: "What's Arizona's favorite joke?"
A: "Ev Mecham."

— The Official Evan Mecham Joke Book

Jokes about politicians are as old as politics, and some of the jokes are probably older. Henri Bergson thought that we laugh at someone in order to chastise him into acting in a more socially acceptable manner. Freud, on the other hand, thought jokes are guilty pleasures in which the anti-social part of our personalities was getting off on breaking the rules. Most people I've talked to say they joke about Mecham because they're just plain embarrassed.

"I'll take a urine test when Ev takes an IQ test," says one familiar bumper sticker.

Local radio announcers at KCLS recorded a parody song called "I Want a New Gov." ("I want a new gov,/ Not a 60s bigot./ Just ask the little pickaninnies,/ If they think good ol' Evan can dig it./ I want a new gov,/ One who knows where it's at,/ One who won't scare the Doobies off,/ And knows the world ain't flat.") Other call-in radio talk shows featured Evan Mecham Joke Days:

> "Last night when the governor and his wife were out to dinner, the waiter asked Flo what she'd like to order, and she said, 'The roast beef, medium rare.' 'French fries or baked potato?' 'Baked.' 'And what about the vegetable?' the waiter asked. 'He'll have the same thing,' Flo answered" (KDKB).

FITZSIMMONS © '87 The Arizona Daily Star

In a paper presented at the International Conference on World Humor, Alleen Nilsen suggested that the volume and tenor of jokes about Arizona's governor indicates that he is in increasing trouble with the electorate. Some samples:

Q: Why does Mecham have to open his mouth?
A: To change feet.

Q: What would be the difference if Mecham and a skunk were run over on the highway?
A: There would be skid marks in front of the skunk.

Q: Why does California have AIDS while Arizona has Mecham?
A: California got first choice.

Dr. Nilsen suggested that hostility may have reached a level beyond humor. "Some of my recent requests for Mecham jokes have been met with such responses as, 'They're not funny anymore,' and 'Mecham IS a joke'" (*Arizona Daily Star*, April 3, 1987).

Nilsen's worries seem to have been premature, for September 1987 saw the publication of *The Official Evan Mecham Joke Book*.

Q: Why does the Governor's plane have so much trouble getting off the ground?
A: It only has a right wing.

Q: Why did Governor Mecham cancel Easter?
A: He found out the eggs were colored.

But more of this later. After all, we're pretending that this book is about things the Governor actually said.

GARY MARKSTEIN *Tribune Newspapers, AZ © 8/87*

BORO *The Phoenix Gazette '86*

II.
Cancelling King

One of Evan Mecham's very first acts as governor of Arizona was to cancel the state's holiday honoring Martin Luther King, Jr. The official, paid holiday for government workers had been illegally created by his predecessor as governor, Bruce Babbitt, Mecham said, pointing to a ruling by State Attorney General Bob Corbin.

Public reaction was immediate and, in the press, almost completely negative. Arizona House Minority Leader Art Hamilton, the ranking black in the Arizona State Legislature, was "flabbergasted," while others were "stunned," "appalled" and "dumbfounded." Mecham responded in *The Arizona Republic* on February 2, 1987:

> "I rescinded the politically motivated, illegally executed order of my predecessor knowing full well that I would be criticized by narrow-minded persons who are totally intolerant of those who disagree with their own biased opinions."

Mecham said the rescission had nothing to do with any personal antagonism toward blacks or toward King, though when asked by *Arizona Trend* magazine he replied:

> "Do I think King, the man, deserves a holiday? No."
>
> January 1987

21

Steve Benson did a great cartoon for *The Arizona Republic*, a drawing of a sample "Referendum Ballot" in which voters got to choose "What Blacks in this state really need:

☐ **another holiday**   ☐ **another governor"**

but Pat Murphy, publisher of the *Republic* (and the *Phoenix Gazette* as well, in case you thought you were reading two different newspapers), for whatever reason, refused to let us reprint any of Benson's stuff, no matter what compensation we offered. *Some people* might conclude that this had something to do with the *Republic*'s sudden change of editorial policy toward Mecham, after a key meeting of the Phoenix 40. . . . But we'd never suggest anything like that without proof.

"The people who want to recognize Martin Luther King can recognize him till the cows come home[.] They can recognize him 365 days out of the year. Why is it so important to force everybody else to recognize it?"

Ev in *Arizona Trends,*
January 1987

Ev attracted a lot of attention because of the King controversy, appearing in *Time, Newsweek, USA Today, People, Rolling Stone, Playboy* and other national publications, and on a number of national television news forums. The governor professed to be baffled by all this fuss, especially by all the fuss over King.

"He's been blown up by others and doesn't deserve a holiday," Ev said about King at a news conference following a roasting on the *MacNeil/Lehrer News Hour.*

Arizona Republic,
January 20, 1987

Ev tried to clarify his concern for minorities:

"What the blacks need is jobs. They don't need another holiday."

Arizona Republic,
January 18, 1987

Apparently misled by the press, people continued to misunderstand the governor's position.

"I'm not a racist, I've got black friends. I employ black people. I don't employ them because they're black. I employ them because they are the best people who applied for the cotton-picking job."

Ev in *Arizona Trend,*
January 1987

23

BORO *The Phoenix Gazette '87*

When the chairwoman of Arizona's "Juneteenth Celebration," an annual commemoration of the end of slavery in Texas, announced that she was breaking with tradition and refusing to invite the governor to read a proclamation at the ceremony, Mecham responded:

> "I think there's a great deal of bigotry in people who claim others are bigots when they have nothing to base it on."
>
> *Phoenix Gazette,*
> June 12, 1987

> "A local joke was that the Pontiac was 'the Mexican Cadillac.' There was no slur intended and no one seemed to mind."
>
> Ev reflecting on his start at
> an Ajo Pontiac Dealership.
> *Come Back America,* p. 21

BORO *The Phoenix Gazette '87*

As if Ev's own book, *Come Back America*, published in 1982 during his fourth unsuccessful bid for the governorship, didn't lend itself readily enough to misinterpretation by detractors, the governor found himself in the position of defending *The Making of America*, by his good friend and mentor Cleon Skousen. Some people felt it was racist because, among other things, it included an essay that referred to blacks as "pickaninnies."

> "It's a good book," Ev explained on ABC's *Good Evening America*. "It uses the word pickaninny in an historical sense."
>
> August 11, 1987

Insensitivity to the implications of using a word like "pickaninnies" seemed to be another "non-issue":

> "As I was a boy growing up, blacks themselves referred to their children as pickaninnies."
>
> *Phoenix Gazette,*
> March 24, 1987

GARY MARKSTEIN *Tribune Newspapers, AZ*

III.
Cancelling Conventions

Unfortunately for the tourist trade in Arizona, reaction to Mecham's cancellation of the King holiday was more than verbal. A number of major entertainers cancelled concerts in the state. Stevie Wonder, U-2, the Doobie Brothers and Luther Vandross were among the acts boycotting the state, while other groups, such as Peter, Paul & Mary and Kool and the Gang donated funds from their Arizona concerts to the movement to recall the governor. (Ron Bellus, Mecham's embattled former press secretary, said he had it on good authority that certain of these groups simply couldn't sell enough tickets and were using the King brouhaha as an excuse to get out of unprofitable engagements.)

Besides, Ev noted philosophically, "We can't lose anything we don't have."

The Arizona Republic,
March 2, 1987

BORO *The Phoenix Gazette '87*

Among the other things Arizona was soon never to have were over fifty conventions that had been booked for the state and subsequently cancelled. These included those of the National Newspaper Publishers Association, the National Urban League, the United Methodist Church and Planned Parenthood. (According to *The Arizona Republic*, June 7, 1987, Mecham announced that his staff had investigated some of the cancellations and found that the groups had never really intended to come to Arizona in the first place.)

Anyway, Ev was unimpressed:

> "I've got some letters in the mail saying, 'We are not going to come to your state.' We also, however, have some that say, 'Thank God for people like you, and we think more of Arizona and we'll be out there.' So . . . that cuts both ways."

> *The Arizona Republic,*
> March 2, 1987

Since revenue losses for the conventions were still estimated at only about twenty million dollars by mid-May, Ev continued to pooh-pooh the furor over King Day:

> "I didn't know there was a furor. A furor is when there was a lot of upset people. There's only a few."

The Arizona Republic,
May 19, 1987

Early in June, *The Arizona Republic* reported that "Planned Parenthood Federation of America has canceled its national convention in Phoenix, prompting Governor Evan Mecham to charge Monday that the group is part of a conspiracy to help boost his recall." Mecham pointed out that other groups, such as the "Association for the Blind," hadn't cancelled.

National media coverage had, by this time, made Evan Mecham Arizona's most exposed governor, easily eclipsing the efforts of presidential hopeful Bruce Babbitt. Doonesbury cartoonist Garry Trudeau, seemed typical of the east-coast bleeding-heart liberals making trouble for Arizona. When Ev investigated suing Trudeau for slander, he was outraged to discover that editorial cartoonists DON'T HAVE TO TELL THE TRUTH about public figures. A supporter on his call-in radio show was quick to point out to the governor that Trudeau at least had portrayed him as young and virile.

Despite the conspiracy, Ev assured the Southern Arizona Innkeepers Association that the state's tourism industry would not be hurt by the King issue. Besides that, where was their pride?

> "Are we such a bunch of wimps that we listen to people who say, 'We're going to come in from the outside and tell you how to run your political machinery in Arizona'? . . . When we start talking about the negatives of all the people that are not going to come to Arizona, I declare that totally a non-issue."

> *The Arizona Republic,*
> June 15, 1987

Ev followed up his remarks by later reassigning the press secretary who'd handled the King controversy as director of advertising and community relations for the state Office of Tourism, and by asking out-of-state conservatives to move to Arizona "to counter the liberal outsiders." (Later Ev denied asking, sort of, maybe. More on this Famous Fund Raising Letter Fiasco later.)

> *Mesa Tribune,*
> September 30, 1987

FITZSIMMONS © '87 The Arizona Daily Star

Things got really serious, finally, when major sports teams began to question Mecham's cancellation of King Day. Talk of an NFL franchise diminished, and plans for holding this year's NFL owners conference in Arizona evaporated. The final insult was cancellation by the National Basketball Association of the league's annual meeting, which had been scheduled for Scottsdale.

> "Well," Ev responded, "I guess they forget how many white people they get coming to watch them play." Ev said the cancellation looked to him like part of that conspiracy again. "Sounds like they've got it pretty well-coordinated, doesn't it? Very definitely."
>
> *The Arizona Republic,*
> June 7, 1987

A reporter from the Douglas, Arizona, *Daily Dispatch* noted that the boos that accompanied Mecham's appearance at the Phoenix Suns game on August 18 provided about the only excitement at the basketball arena that night.

FITZSIMMONS © '87 The Arizona Daily Star

Finally Ev could only respond to the King "rhubarb,"

"I'm totally sick of it."

The Arizona Republic,
July 4, 1987

He declared a Sunday as a King holiday.

GARY MARKSTEIN © 7/87 Tribune Newspapers, AZ

IV.
Cancelling Ev

By the time the Recall campaign was officially allowed to begin, the idea was so popular that organizers were able to hold a fund raising lottery to see who would be allowed to sign first. Of course a lot of Democrats liked the idea, for their own selfish reasons. U.S. Representative Morris Udall said he supported the Recall because Mecham "is hurting the state. In fact, he's been an unmitigated disaster for the people of Arizona" (*The Arizona Republic*, July 22, 1987). Bruce Babbitt called Mecham proof that Darwin was wrong (*The Arizona Republic*, September 23, 1987).

> Ev was amused by the Recall leaders. He said, "I love their optimism."
>
> *Tempe Tribune*,
> July 22, 1987

He was "unconcerned." He "just considered the source."

> These critics are just "rabid left-wingers who really want to give me a rash."
>
> quoted in *Newsweek*,
> March 9, 1987

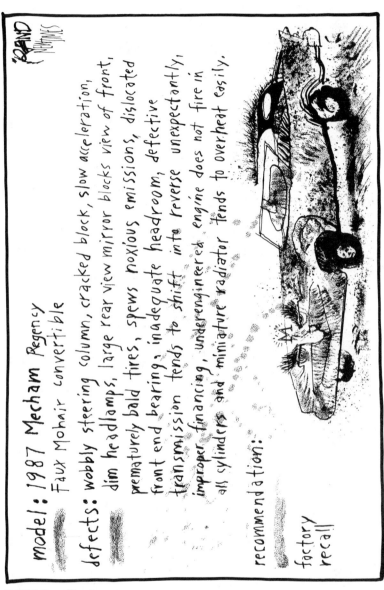

model: 1987 Mecham Regency
Faux Mohair convertible

defects: wobbly steering column, cracked block, slow acceleration, dim headlamps, large rear view mirror blocks view of front, prematurely bald tires, spews noxious emissions, dislocated front end bearing, inadequate headroom, defective transmission tends to shift into reverse unexpectantly, improper financing, underengineered engine does not fire in all cylinders and miniature radiator tends to overheat easily.

recommendation:

factory
recall

Burton Kruglick, GOP party boss in Arizona and, according to *The Arizona Republic,* a Designated Mecham Mouthpiece, helped put the finger on Recall leaders, in order to prevent concern among the general public that there might be real issues involved:

> They are, Kruglick said, "a band of homo-sexuals and a few dissident Democrats."
>
> *The Arizona Republic,*
> July 8, 1987

Did Ev himself intend that? When asked about the Recall now, he said,

> "If a band of homosexuals and a few dissi-dent Democrats can do that, why, heavens, the state deserves what it gets."
>
> *The Arizona Republic,*
> July 7, 1987

He did not say whether the same people were gay and rabid, judiciously leaving it to readers to draw their own conclusions. However, a flier circulated by a Mecham support group warned that recall-petition signers could get AIDS from handling the ink pens used by those collecting signatures (*The Arizona Republic,* September 30, 1987).

BORO *The Phoenix Gazette '87*

When his own party members began to attack him in the State Legislature, Mecham assured the press that their spokesman "just wants publicity" (*The Arizona Republic*, July 21, 1987).

> After all, Ev noted, "I'm the best thing that ever happened to the Republican Party."
>
> *The Arizona Republic*,
> July 21, 1987

As Mecham's counterattacks shot off more and more Republican feet, more and more Republicans began to complain. Former State GOP Chairman Tom Pappas confessed, "I'm just totally losing the faith, and it's only [by] pure party loyalty that I'm hanging on" (*Mesa Tribune*, October 1, 1987).

Republican Representative Chris Herstam said, after receiving a Mecham fund-raising letter, "As a Republican, I'm very disappointed in the letter. It contained many insensitive comments and it demonstrates a severe case of paranoia" (*Mesa Tribune*, October 1, 1987).

GARY MARKSTEIN © *Tribune Newspapers, AZ*

Like King Day, the Recall was apparently another "non-issue." "Why should I be worried about it? There's no substance to it," Ev had responded earlier to newspaper reports of eroding public support (*The Arizona Republic*, May 15, 1987).

Ev seemed to feel that even Democrats had no real bones to pick with him. "They just don't have enough work to do, so they have to find somebody to try to harass. I really don't pay any attention to them, so they lose their total effect on me," he responded when Dems charged that his TV advertising and home mailings ought to be considered campaign expenditures (*Mesa Tribune*, September 24, 1987).

GARY MARKSTEIN © *Tribune Newspapers, AZ*

Mecham remained convinced that the main thrust behind the Recall movement was being provided by homosexuals, perhaps because Recall originator Ed Buck was a professed homosexual and wasn't a Dissident Democrat. Politics may make strange bedfellows, and Ev was adamant on THAT issue. When a caller to his radio talk show tried to convince him that homosexuals were a substantial part of the electorate, Ev pooh-poohed the notion, and asked for a list of names. (He later clarified that he didn't want to do anything in particular with the list.) When another caller claimed to be a homosexual member of Ev's own Church of the Latter Day Saints, Ev was adamant that the man was mistaken in his beliefs:

> "The church I belong to does not allow homosexuals to participate under any circumstances. It is not . . . an alternative lifestyle. It is not an acceptable lifestyle."
>
> "Talk With the Governor,"
> KTAR Radio, February 12, 1987

Gays were naturally concerned about Ev's politics. Ev didn't think gays had the rights they thought they had, as typified by his suggestion to the president of Arizona State University that membership of gay clubs among student organizations was fostering an unlawful lifestyle. On the other hand, he thought they were unreasonable to be upset since, if they DID have the constitutional rights they claimed they had, they had nothing to worry about. Anyway, Ev didn't think much of those rights himself. In clarifying what he'd meant in his inaugural address by his pledge to "wipe out discrimination," he noted:

> "I don't think gay rights have anything to do with discrimination. I do not believe that is a legitimate alternative lifestyle. . . . When I talk about discrimination, I talk about race, color, creed. When you start talking about gay rights, you start talking about the moral issues and that's certainly a whole different ball game."
>
> *Scottsdale Progress,*
> January 6, 1987

> "In a day and age when militant gay leaders are feeding the nation a steady diet of their 'alternative lifestyles' and they stand before the nightly news cameras demanding the taxpayers pay for their AIDS treatments, I feel it is important for conservatives to stand up for traditional American values."
>
> — from a Mecham fundraising letter quoted in the *Mesa Tribune,*
> September 30, 1987

48

BORO *The Phoenix Gazette '87*

The Committee to Recall the Governor frequently noted that Ev Mecham was their greatest benefactor. A favorite conspiracy of both sides was an anti-Recall letter sent out by the governor's office that raised thousands of dollars for Ev and thousands of signatures for the Recall.

Mailed at the end of September under the Governor's letterhead and bearing his signature, this four-pager said, in part:

> "I want you to sell your house, pack your belongings, quit your job and come to [Arizona . . . to] help counter the liberal outsiders who are preparing to spend millions against me. . . .
>
> "Without your contribution I will risk being crushed by the millions of dollars the militant liberals and the homosexual lobby plan to spend against me."

Mecham's *new* press secretary said that Mecham had approved the letter, but Mecham later said his signature machine had been used on it without his prior approval. While he believed "there isn't anything wrong with the overall message itself," he apparently thought the wording could have been improved: "It isn't like I'd say it" (*Mesa Tribune, The Arizona Republic*, October 1, 1987).

GARY MARKSTEIN *Tribune Newspapers* © 1987

51

GARY MARKSTEIN © *Tribune Newspapers, AZ*

As usual, the sex thing got more attention than some people thought it deserved. When Donna Carlson, a top Mecham aide, was questioned about her passing out bumper stickers at the State Capitol that read "Queer Ed Buck's Recall," she denied it was a personal attack on Buck, saying it was just "a cute play on words" (*The Arizona Republic,* May 25, 1987).

Homosexuality continued to be a major defense against the Recall, until the Phoenix Gazette decided to report that "Ken Shippy, the teenage founder of the Ev Mecham Fan Club, resigned from his volunteer job in the governor's office . . . after it was revealed he is a convicted child molestor."

> "We're not distancing ourselves from Kip," Mecham's Press Secretary clarified. "We never really opened our arms to him."
>
> *Phoenix Gazette,*
> July 8, 1987

Burton Kruglick was taken aback when someone suggested it was now time to stop disparaging the sexual proclivities of both sides and deal with the real issues of the Recall. Kip Shippy is "a nice young man," Kruglick responded. "He's corrected himself. He's not doing it anymore. I don't see how you can compare this to someone who's a homosexual and continues to be a homosexual" (*Phoenix Gazette,* July 9, 1987).

RAND *New Times*

The press, at least, seemed to feel differently. But then, it seems, the press had been the REAL cause of the Recall movement all along.

THE A[...]

Mecham and the press:
Was it murder or suicide?

By Pat Murphy
Republic Big Shot

PHOENIX—No one expected the extreme measures which confronted the [...]

DON'T JUST GET MAD ARIZONA, GET EVAN!

RAND New Times

V.
Pressing Mecham

"I'm not really against the press. They've had more fun with me than anybody in the history of the state."

Ev Mecham,
The Arizona Republic,
January 31, 1987

Ev Mecham declared April 1 to be "Press Corpse Appreciation Day." When asked by reporters for a portrait of himself to hang in the press room at the Capitol, he asked if they'd like one made of cork so that they could throw darts at it (*Arizona Daily Sun,* April 3, 1987). But relations between the governor and the press haven't always been that jovial.

BORO *The Phoenix Gazette '87*

From the beginning of his campaign for governor, Mecham accused the press of being biased for the other side, whoever the other side happened to be at the time. (To counteract this, Mecham published his own tabloid newspaper twice during the campaign, each time managing to swing crucial votes at just the right time. Perhaps jealousy is at the heart of press hostility to Mecham; if they'd been half as successful swaying public opinion as he'd been, Ev would never have been elected.)

When the media continued their "Mecham-bashing" after he'd become governor, Ev responded with his own radio call-in show, frequent television appearances, and another home-mailed tabloid, *The Governor's Report to the People of Arizona.* Besides illuminating articles on "Mr. 65" himself, informing us how Ev was responsible for giving the nation back its Real Speed Limit, and reprints of a number of supportive articles, such as

"Mecham Suffers from Selective Reporting,"

it was chock-full of weighty fillers like the ones on the following page.

These apparently had no connection to the bold-face "throw-away" filler on the front-page of the July/August issue of the state employees newsletter advising workers to support their boss or find another job: "If you work for a man, in heaven's name work for him . . . , speak well of him and stand by the institution he represents. . . . If you must vilify, condemn and eternally disparage—resign your position." That, newsletter editor Claudia Smith informed reporters, was purely coincidental and not intended to put pressure on anyone, much less to refer directly to the governor (*The Arizona Republic,* July 23, 1987).

BORO *The Phoenix Gazette '87*

"Don't worry about imitators. While they're following in your tracks, they can't pass you."

"Husband coming home: 'What a day! The computer broke down and we all had to think!'"

"What a lot of people are looking for these days is less to do, more time to do it in, and higher pay for not getting it done in the first place."

In the meantime, the press continued to poke fun in tender places. *The Arizona Republic* reported that "a public-relations aide in state government was asked a touchy question about Governor Evan Mecham. The reporter also asked, 'Am I putting you out on a limb?' 'If I answer,' said the aide, 'you're putting me out on the street.'"

— January 31, 1987

Mecham's relationship with the press, in Phoenix in particular, escalated to the level where Ev effectively banned *Phoenix Gazette* reporter John Kolbe from his news conferences and offices:

> "As far as I'm concerned, he's a non-person. I don't want to even recognize his existence. . . . I think if you would read his writings over a number of years, you would say that there comes a time when there is a particular person in the news media whose writings have no redeeming value whatsoever to inform the readers with anything worthwhile to read relating to some subjects. I'm one of those subjects."
>
> *Phoenix Gazette,*
> March 3, 1987

Apparently Ev never thought of declaring himself a non-subject.

Although informed by the Attorney General's Office that he might not have the authority to actually make someone a "non-person" (apparently that was a legislative function), Ev persisted. When gossip columnist Gail Tabor criticized his wife Florence for her attire at an official reception in Nicaragua, the Governor created her his First Female Non-Person (*The Arizona Republic,* June 4, 1987).

BORO *The Phoenix Gazette '87*

63

Apparently even video cameras failed to capture the Reel Truth. The following exchange was filmed by a number of television stations and parts were aired on local stations, the CBS Evening News and other national programs.

[As our camera pans, *Arizona Republic* reporter Sam Stanton accosts Governor Evan Mecham, who is just leaving a press conference.] "Governor, we've gotten several different stories here. Can you tell us what the true version is?"

[Mecham wheels, marches back, and jabs his finger in Stanton's face. He has to reach up a considerable distance.] "You hadn't better say what the truth is."

Stanton, surprised: "I'm not saying —"

Mecham interrupting: "Don't you — you are questioning my integrity. I gave you the statement, I gave you the statement."

Stanton: "I am certainly not [questioning your integrity], Governor."

Mecham: "Don't ever ask me for a true statement again!"

dialogue reprinted in
The Arizona Republic,
September 30, 1987

Evan continued the following day on KTAR radio, "Nobody calls me a liar, particularly a reporter from *The Arizona Republic,* as unaccustomed to truth as they are." Nobody but Evan maybe.

GARY MARKSTEIN *Tribune Newspapers* © 3/87

66

The national media was no kinder. Other than a fetching beef-cake photo of Ev reclining on a diving board in *People Magazine,* no one showed the slightest interest in getting to know the real Ev.

Ev's special assistant, Sam Steiger, a man who says he just "likes to piss people off" anyway, had his own words for reporters when they failed to understand how the gov's creation of a new state department called "The Arizona Drug Control Service" was "not [the formation of] a new department":

> "I don't know how you can tell that to a reporter, because that takes more than one sentence, and there are a lot of 3 and 4 syllable words in it."
>
> *The Arizona Republic,*
> February 12, 1987

Some people just don't seem to know what's funny and what isn't. When a caller to his radio show complained that the governor was the laughingstock of the country and had embarrassed the people of Arizona on a national television appearance, Ev replied,

> "You and people like you and some elements of the liberal press are actually the only laughingstock."
>
> "Talk to the Governor,"
> KTAR,
> February 28, 1987

GARY MARKSTEIN

VI.
All the Governor's Men (and Girls)

Q: What do Mecham's political appointees have in common?
A: Parole officers.

— *The Official Evan Mecham Joke Book*

The people Evan Mecham appointed or nominated for office under his administration were a constant source of controversy for the new governor.

On the one hand, there was Mecham's contention that the press ought to have something better to do than dig into a man's past and print picky, picky, picky stuff that his original victims had probably forgiven or forgotten long ago. On the other hand, there was Mecham's own campaign slogan:

"Integrity is the issue."

In the area of education, Ev's appointees reflect some of his own views on the propriety of teaching things like sex education and the theory of evolution with tax-payers' money. A popular idea in the administration was to push through a bill that would allow the teaching of evolution only on the same "theoretical" basis on which creationism is taught. Ev summed it up this way, much to the mystification of some English teachers:

"If you're going to teach either one, you teach them both as theory. You should not leave it as a vacuum."

"Talk to the Governor,"
KTAR,
February 12, 1987

BORO *The Phoenix Gazette '87*

70

His appointees knew when to take a cue:

> "If a student wants to say the world is flat, the teacher doesn't have the right to try to prove otherwise. . . . The schools don't have any business telling people what to believe."

Jim Cooper, Mecham's education advisor, before the House Education Committee, *The Arizona Republic*, February 5, 1987

Ada Thomas, a housewife Mecham appointed to the Education Commission, boasted raising several children as her qualifications. She voted "no" on several sex education publications and programs because some failed to overtly condemn homosexuality and another defined "masturbation." When she was informed these publications were to be provided not to students but to parents, she replied that such things were "not even good for parents" to read (*The Arizona Republic*, April 28, 1987). One publication reported that Ms. Thomas insists that sex education should not include naming parts of the body.

Ev defended Ada's views as a member of the Arizona Eagle Forum, "a group organized to fight against the women's movement."

> "She made a statement that . . . working women increase divorce. I believe that is a given fact, but that doesn't mean we're going to tell anybody how to live their lives."

"Talk To the Governor,"
KTAR,
March 28, 1987

Many of Ev's appointments appeared to be purely compensation for favors owed.

Bill Long, a home builder, became Mecham's chairman of the Arizona Commission on the Arts, though thus far in his tenure his most significant action seems to have been hiring Mail Marketing Agency, which wrote advertising copy for Ev's fund raising (*The Arizona Republic*, September 30, 1987).

Tom Wilmeth, the top ad seller for Ev's tabloid, *The Governor's Report to the People of Arizona*, was appointed to a newly created post to run the Department of Corrections Juvenile Facility. The governor's office maintained that Wilmeth was qualified because he had a master's degree in education. When asked about this appointment, Ev's press secretary responded that the appointment did not show "a one-to-one correlation to his work," and Mecham denied that he had asked anyone to make the appointment. Sam Steiger, the gov's special assistant, was quick to contradict: "I was told by the governor to get him that job."

Mesa Tribune,
October 1, 1987

The loudest cries went up when Ev insisted on giving his old friend Fred Craft a million dollar state contract to serve as Arizona's lobbyist for the multi-billion dollar federal "Super-Collider Project" — after the specially organized state selection panel rejected Craft and the federal agency to award the contract had already listed him as unsuitable. According to newspaper interviews with all the members of the panel willing to talk (four out of five), Mecham threatened to withdraw his support for the project unless Craft got the job.

After Craft had been rejected by the Legislature, Mecham hired him anyway as his D.C. lobbyist and paid him out of his administrative fund, all without consulting the Arizona congressional delegation.

Arizona Republic,
Phoenix Gazette,
July 3, 1987

72

BORO *The Phoenix Gazette '87*

FITZSIMMONS © 87 The Arizona Daily Star

74

Ev's most famous nominees were never appointed:

William Heuisler withdrew his candidacy for the post of "Special Investigator of Waste and Corruption in Government" when it was revealed that, in applying for his private investigator's license, he had failed to list his court-martial convictions for "wrongful appropriation of property" and for abusing a prisoner, as well as his disorderly conduct conviction for fighting with a Tucson policeman (*The Arizona Republic*, January 22, 1987).

Alberto Rodriguez was Mecham's nominee for liquor superintendant, even after he admitted knowing about and belonging to a Douglas club that had been raided by state agents for illegal gambling. The catch: Rodriguez had been mayor at the time. While Rodriguez was being considered for the position, he was also under investigation as a suspect in an active, if ancient, murder investigation.

> "I think Al will do a good job of enforcement," Ev said. "He's highly qualified, and his training, his background, everything, is very good."
>
> *The Arizona Republic*,
> January 23, 1987

> Concerning Rex Waite, his choice for Director of the Department of Revenue, Ev said, "Rex is very well-positioned in the business world. Normally we wouldn't be able to entice a man of his qualifications with the salary we're willing to pay."

Waite, whose Southwestern Bank had failed in 1981, was currently owner of an ice cream store.

> KTAR,
> February 28, 1987

75

Word got out that Ev had asked Joe Haldiman III, who'd had his insurance license revoked for misappropriation of funds and was still under investigation by the Attorney General, to help select the head of the division that insures the state government.

Ted Hume was appointed to head the Residential Utility Consumer Office despite his notoriously pro-utility positions. One of his first acts was to fire the agency's head attorney during his cross-examination of utility officials in a rate-increase hearing.

Then Ev appointed Tex Barron, former general manager of Rillito Race Track in Tucson, to oversee dog and horse racing.

To be fair (and don't ask me why yet), at least one of Ev's appointees didn't seem political at all. After being criticized for his insensitivity to minorities, Ev decided to hire former beauty queen and weather lady Zoe Soto as his liaison to the Hispanic community.

> "I was so dazzled by her beauty that I just hired her on the spot," the governor declared. Unfortunately, Ms. Soto was not a U.S. citizen, and Ev was in violation of a state hiring law.
>
> *Arizona Republic,*
> July 24, 1987

When Senate Republicans asked Ev to confer with them on his appointments to avoid future embarrassment, Ev told them it was none of their business whom he hired. So *they* decided to hire a private investigator to check the backgrounds of Ev's appointments.

> *Arizona Republic,*
> January 25, 1987

Doonesbury

BY GARRY TRUDEAU

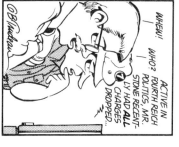

DOONESBURY COPYRIGHT 1987
G. B. Trudeau.
Reprinted with the permission of Universal
Press Syndicate. All rights reserved.

With Sam Steiger as Ev's special assistant (and, some said, chief strategist), it's a wonder that Republicans could have been even faintly surprised by any of this. Known for brandishing guns at enemies who sometimes mistook Sam's innocent behavior for threats, Steiger once shot a neighbor's burros because the animals trespassed on his range. Only Mecham could have arranged enough of that sort of excitement in an administration to keep someone like Steiger from stealing all the headlines in Section B.

When Ev nominated Russell Ritchie to be Revenue Director, he assured everyone,

> "There isn't a thing about this man that isn't just squeaky clean. . . . He hasn't done anything that's a problem for the whole world to know about."
>
> *The Arizona Republic,*
> April 7, 1987

Turned out that this nominee for head tax collector was under investigation by the Attorney General's Office, the firm he had worked for had had its operating license revoked, and he had filed his 1985 tax return more than a year late. (Acting Revenue Director Michael Wolfe, who reported this infraction, was fired the following day. Guess Ev was serious when he said the whole world didn't need to know about that problem.)

> *The Arizona Republic,*
> April 7, 1987

BORO *The Phoenix Gazette '87*

GARY MARKSTEIN © Tribune Newspapers 1987

VII.
The World According to Ev

"I will work in cooperation instead of confrontation. Confrontation isn't strength. Confrontation is not leadership getting along with people in accomplishing a purpose."

Ev in *Arizona Trend*,
January 1987

Evan Mecham sees himself as a Constitutionalist, a man dedicated to preserving and enhancing the basic tenets of the Constitution which have been steadily eroded since the advent of the New Deal. (Well, maybe a little earlier, since Ev advocated the repeal of the Sixteenth Amendment in his book *Come Back America*. That particular amendment from 1913 legalized federal income tax. So, I never said the guy was all bad.)

In fact, Evan feels that the Constitution was religiously inspired, and that "America came into being because God in heaven wanted his children to be free, and so he raised up a special group of people that he sent to this Earth" (*The Arizona Republic*, May 18, 1987). People saw him pause for a long time during his inauguration speech; Ev was waiting for a similar kind of divine inspiration. Judging by the results. . . .

The basic problem with American government today, as Ev told the John Birch Society (no, he's not a member, even if his wife was; it's just "one of a number of groups of people across the country that are concerned about America and I join them in that concern"), the trouble with America is that we've strayed a little too far from the actual intentions of our Founding Fathers:

> "I'm not sure but what maybe we have become a bit too much of a democracy," he told the National Guard Association of Arizona while discussing on the 200th Anniversary of the Constitution.
>
> *The Arizona Republic,*
> June 1, 1987

FITZSIMMONS © 87 *The Arizona Daily Star*

FITZSIMMONS © 87 The Arizona Daily Star

Our system of justice hasn't fared any better. To rectify that and better implement his anti-drug campaign, Ev proposed to the Legislature that he be allowed to appoint temporary Superior Court judges to handle drug-related cases, set up a judicial oversight committee that would be exempt from open-meeting and open-record law requirements, remove the state's chief justice and two lay members from the Criminal Justice Commission, and send the National Guard to seal off the Mexican Border (*Arizona Daily Sun*, March 9, 1987).

The mandatory sentences he proposed for first offenders seemed a little stiff to some, especially considering that his own contacts with the law had sometimes been less than satisfactory. After the Arizona Supreme Court awarded over ten thousand dollars in damages to a woman who had bought a car from him, Ev exclaimed, "I've never seen such a total miscarriage of justice in my life" (*Phoenix Gazette*, December 18, 1986).

FITZSIMMONS © 87 The Arizona Daily Star

Another problem with the government is that it regulates the wrong things. As he'd "proven" in his book *Come Back America,* there really is no need at all for an Environmental Protection Agency:

> "I lived in the copper-producing town of Ajo for four years. I never heard of anyone getting sick or contracting any disease because of smelter smoke."

On the other hand, nobody seems willing to do anything about things that really are killing us, like pornography:

> "It's easy to take the cop-out . . . that [pornography is] a victimless crime. It's convenient when you get the wrong kind of judges, and we've got a lot of wrong judges. . . . We can't make [the definition of obscenity] an individual decision. We have to have laws to wipe it out. . . . These forces that want to bring moral degradation continually go on the basis that they're using freedom."

> Ev addressing the Citizens for
> Decency through Law, Inc.

Since his reputation for decisive solutions to social problems had preceded him, it became necessary for Ev to clarify a suggestion he'd made before the Citizens for Decency that the easiest way to get rid of an adult bookstore would be to run a Mack truck through it:

> "I'm kidding about the Mack truck.
> I never seriously thought about it. I did think about it, but not seriously."

> *Phoenix Gazette,*
> March 1987

There is a solid foundation to Ev's philosophy of government: religion. As he put it, most impressively, in *Come Back America*,

> "There is a religious foundation to all ideas
> of governance that rise above tyranny."

Such eloquence about religion raised the hopes of his supporters that he really would be able to use the occasion of Pope John Paul's visit to Phoenix to bolster his image. When a caller to his "Talk to the Governor" show asked him just three days before the visit what he planned to say to the Pope upon greeting him, Ev replied,

> "Golly, I don't know. I don't know whether
> he speaks English or not."
>
> KTAR,
> September 11, 1987

The Governor informed the reporters that he was glad the Pope spoke English, because the only Latin he knew was "Ootfray Oopslay."

NED S © '87

89

BORO *The Phoenix Gazette '87*

"Ev Mecham doesn't like the idea of communists parked in his nation's back yard."

*The Governor's Report to
the People of Arizona,*
September 1987

In the arena of foreign policy, Ev has been as effective as elsewhere, despite the fact that few of his predecessors in state government had ever bothered even to make foreign policy.

But not everybody appreciated Ev's efforts. "The idea is ludicrous, even for him," was Mo Udall's response to Ev's decision to send Arizona's National Guard to fight communism in Honduras. "The whole thing ought to be abandoned as harebrained and dangerous."

In *Come Back America,* Ev observed that education was the key to rescuing America from the Usurpers. "It is obvious that there are many honest people misled into following the usurpers bent on total control of this nation even if it meant destroying it in the process."

After all, it would be confusing if the majority of all Americans were actually in on the conspiracy, so he concluded that most of us simply needed to be re-educated.

> "The schools," he said, "have neglected their duty to teach the Constitutional system of government. Had they done so, the people would not have fallen for the false doctrine of Socialism and we would not be in the trouble we were in. It stands to reason, then, that the way to awaken enough people to correct the problems is to educate them in correct principles."

But where does one start with reeducation? Certainly not with federally approved educational programs.

> "In the opinion of educators I know federal intrusion has been the principal cause of deterioration in the quality of education in America."

Mecham Aide Mac Matheson told first graders who wrote to the governor regarding the holiday for Martin Luther King:

> "The governor is not impressed by letters, cards and posters prepared by students influenced by curriculum materials distributed by the National Education Association, which, to say the least, presents a highly biased image of the slain civil rights leader."

> *The Arizona Republic,*
> March 1, 1987

GARY MARKSTEIN © 1987 Tribune Newspapers Copley News Service

FITZSIMMONS © '87 The Arizona Daily Star

94

Probably the governor's right.

We do need reeducation.

And the governor could use a little input too. As he put it himself,

> "I haven't been getting any positive criticism from anyone."

Arizona Republic,
July 23, 1987

✂

ORDER FORM

Send check, money order, or cash (as if you had some reason to trust us) to:

World According to E.M.
Blue Sky Press
4406 E. Main St.
Suite 102-97
Mesa, AZ 85205

The World According to Evan Mecham is $4.95 a copy, $5.50 if you'd like it autographed by the author. Gift copies can be sent directly to friends or enemies, inscribed:

"Dear _____,

[Your Name] paid me to send you this.

MS"

We'll pay 4th class, domestic postage.

Just fill this out and send the loot:

Name _____

Street Address _____

City _____ State _____ Zip _____

Mail orders will be filled within two days of receipt of your order.

ORDER FORM

Send check, money order, or cash (as if you had some reason to trust us) to:

World According to E.M.
Blue Sky Press
4406 E. Main St.
Suite 102-97
Mesa, AZ 85205

The World According to Evan Mecham is $4.95 a copy, $5.50 if you'd like it autographed by the author. Gift copies can be sent directly to friends or enemies, inscribed:

"Dear _____,
[Your Name] paid me to send you this.
MS"

We'll pay 4th class, domestic postage.

Just fill this out and send the loot:

Name _____

Street Address _____

City _____ State _____ Zip _____

Mail orders will be filled within two days of receipt of your order.